YOU ARE HERE

YOU ARE HERE

Poems New & Old

Leon Stokesbury

The University of Arkansas Press
Fayetteville ✱ 2016

Manufactured in the United States of America

ISBN: 978-1-68226-007-4 (paper)
e-ISBN: 978-1-61075-592-4

20 19 18 17 16 5 4 3 2 1

Designed by Liz Lester

∞ The paper used in this publication meets the minimum requirements of the American National Standard for Permanence of Paper for Printed Library Materials Z39.48-1984.

Library of Congress Control Number: 2016931015

For Susan

"Like to the lark at break of day arising"

CONTENTS

II ✷ AUTUMN RHYTHM (1996)

III ✷ THE DRIFTING AWAY (1986)

ACKNOWLEDGMENTS

Many of the poems in *You Are Here* have been selected from *Often in Different Landscapes* (Austin, 1976), copyright 1976 by Leon Stokesbury; *The Drifting Away* (Fayetteville, 1986), copyright 1986 by Leon Stokesbury; and *Autumn Rhythm* (Fayetteville, 1996), copyright 1996 by Leon Stokesbury.

Grateful acknowledgment is made to the following publications in which some of the poems in *You Are Here: Poems New & Old* originally appeared, some in slightly different versions: *American Literary Review, The Antioch Review, Atlanta Review, Barataria Review, Charlotte Poetry Review, Crazyhorse, The Georgia Review, Greensboro Review, Intro 2, Kentucky Poetry Review, The Kenyon Review, Lowlands Review, Mill Mountain Review, Mississippi Review, New England Review, New Letters, New Orleans Review, New Virginia Review, The New Yorker, Ohio State University Journal, Pacific Review, The Partisan Review, Poem, Poetry Northwest, Prairie Schooner, Quarterly West, Quartet Magazine, Red Weather, River Styx, Shenandoah, Southern Poetry Review, The Southern Review, Stone Drum, Swallow's Tale*, and *Tar River Poetry*.

The poem "Watching My Mother Take Her Last Breath" was chosen to be reprinted from *The Georgia Review* in the *2012 Pushcart Prize XXXVI Best of the Small Presses. Often in Different Landscapes* was selected as a cowinner of the Associated Writing Programs' first Annual Poetry Book Competition in 1975. *Autumn Rhythm* was awarded the Poets' Prize for 1996 as the best book of poetry published by an American that year.

YOU ARE HERE

I ✷ THESE DAYS

Everybody knows the boat is leaking.
Everybody knows the captain lied.

—Leonard Cohen

Nemerov's "A Primer of the Daily Round" Held as a Mirror up to Nature

A peels an apple, while B kneels to God . . .

What, for instance, do you suppose might prove to be
the significance if I were to dismiss class fifteen minutes
early tonight, and each of you, as you stride out
into the descending purple cloaks of dim and gloom,
each of you reaching your separate parking lots
just a bit lighter, because of this slight but sudden
surprising slip of time, each of you igniting
your Probes, Infinitis, Mirages, and Charades,
and tooling back into traffic beneath the Cimmerian dusk—
what, now, might the import prove to be,
as you stream toward your diverse destinations
surrounded by a completely different array of vehicles
than if I had set you free at the usual 7:30
rather than at 7:15?
                                        And what consequence might
you claim if the car in the lane next to you, odd car,
bad car, old Chevy Malibu, swerves into your lane
creating a decidedly unpleasant union and—
in the same way a concrete bust of Elvis placed upon
a three-foot concrete pedestal in your own backyard
becomes the emerald ivy that it's set among,
and like the October umbra of oak and pine that
concrete bust of Elvis rests beneath becomes that bust
of Elvis in return—your bumpers intertwine,
commingling beneath the bleak, black sky?

And as you stumble enraged from your, say, cream
blue Avalon, you see with such clarity the immediately

beloved other—trembling, stunned, numb—not at all
the jousting argumentative you had pre-conceived,
and as you stand there, lonely two, at the murky center
of an empty ocean, exchanging State Farm insurance cards,
telephone numbers too, you hold the two cards
in your hand, side by side, thinking these insurance cards
are like these cars, conjunctive, these cars like the two
of us, or they could be, couldn't they, you think,
and cast a quick glimpse as she slides, but slowly, back
inside: Latin eyes and lashes, looking down, skin
shining, silk beneath her rusty Malibu's interior lighting—
things can become analogous, can't they, by being
placed in tandem, just by happening in a line.
                                                                        You
want only to forgive her, now, to let her know she
has already been forgiven, and to ask her to forgive
you, not for what you've done, but what you would do
someday, in some distant year, distant town, grit
in the bed, the incessantly noisy motel ice machine
across the hall—and for a second you are sure she
would, if you asked, if only you were not too yaller-
yaller-yaller-bellied to begin. Why, even art holds up
such random linkages, you almost say*: Hail in August,*
Landscape With Summer Snow, Desert Rain.
                                                                    But
the moment is gone, ephemeral, little powdery flecks
of glaze falling off the doughnut of the world. *Young*
Man With Thumb Up Butt. And now she is smiling,
apologizing again. O my contiguous, you think, O
my juxtaposed!
                    She looks down once more, then drives
away pocked and pounded, but able, it seems, to negotiate

her path amongst the massive, dark turbidity. And thus
it begins. A week goes by. Your nerve returns. Then
you do call; ask her to dinner. And a year goes by
before you marry, and then nine years, ten years total
from this very night, from my releasing you into
the desultory caprice of evening, O my adjacents,
ten years before the blood and public pain and lies
and her living somewhere close to Albuquerque last
you heard. But still you remember those long lashes
looking down: *Still Life With Red Pepper*: handing you
her State Farm insurance card, as if it were this very
night, tonight, which it is, the vision undiminished,
strong, like that lingering zing left on the tongue
from a more-than-acceptable Gorgonzola—
and then it is you recall this lecture, remember
these fifteen minutes, discerning what consequence
might be claimed: nightshade, scimitar, guillotine,
what future plans for gunfire brought to bear.

So,

go now, my tangentials, wind your weary ways
out amidst this mere shank of the gloaming,
children in an autumn garden, orphans in a storm,
with night dew dripping off the wilting topiary—
some toward domiciles, some to perform your brazen
stand-ups and sit-downs in the gin joints of your choosing—
little molten ingots marching as to war, two by two,
considering, perhaps, the essential nature of side meat
to the American breakfast. Green eggs and ham.
The comic genius of Curly Howard. *Nude at the Window,*
Study in Burnt Sienna. The Menaced Assassin.
The Persistence of Memory. Twilight's Last Gleam.

The Day Kennedy Died

Suppose that on the day Kennedy died
you had a vision. But this was no inner movie
with a discernible plot or anything like it.
Not even very visual when you get down
to admitting to what actually occurred.
About two-thirds through 4th period
Senior Civics, fifteen minutes before
the longed-for lunchtime, suppose you
stood up for no good reason—no reason
at all really—and announced, to the class
and to yourself, "Something. Something
is happening. Something . . . coming. I
can see . . . something. I can see. I . . ."

And that was all. You stood there: blank.
The class roared. Even Phyllis Hoffpaur, girl
most worshipped by you from afar that year,
turned a vaguely pastel shade of red
and smiled, and Richard Head, your best friend,
Dick Head to the chosen few, pulled you down
to your desk whispering, "Jesus, man! Jesus
Christ!" Then you went numb. You did not know
what had occurred. But thirty minutes later,
when Stella (despised) Vandenburg, teacher
of twelfth-grade English, came sashaying
into the cafeteria, informing, left and right,
as many digesting members of the student body
as she could of what she had just heard,
several students began to glance back at you,

remembering what you'd said. A few pointed,
whispering to their confederates, and on that
disturbing day they moved away in the halls.
Even Dick Head did not know what to say.

In 5th period Advanced Math, Principal
Crawford played the radio over the intercom
and the school dropped deeper into history.
For the rest of that day, everyone moved away—
except for the one moment Phyllis Hoffpaur
stared hard, the look on her face asking,
assuming you would know, "Will it be ok?"

And you did not know. No one knew.
Everyone wandered back to their houses
that evening aimless and lost, not knowing,
but certainly sensing something had been
changed forever. *Silsbee High Forever!*
That is our claim! Never, no Never!
Will we lose our fame! you often sang.
But this was to be the class of 1964,
afraid of the future at last, who would select,
as the class song, Terry Stafford's "Suspicion."
And this was November—even in Texas
the month of failings, month of sorrows—
from which there was no turning.
It would be a slow two-month slide until
the manic beginnings of The British Invasion,
three months before Clay's ascension to the throne,
but all you saw walking home that afternoon
were the gangs of gray leaves clotting the curbs
and culverts, the odors of winter forever
in the air: cold, damp, bleak, dead, dull:
dragging you toward the solstice like a tide.

My Wife's Camera Bag
and the Fuji Camera Card Inside It

The museum throng at least five or six deep
jammed up against the velvet rope, with maybe
a quarter of them clicking and clicking
while the guards kept entreating, "No photo,
s'il vous plaît!," to no avail, "Non! Attention!"
and I pushing us to the front, getting between
the guards and her, allowing a couple
of seconds for a decent shot. "Non!"
That gone. "Non!" And gone the back
and buttocks of *The Thinker* as our bus rolled by,
and the huge gilt clock dropping down
from the ceiling of the Musée d'Orsay;
the yellow sunlight gone, glinting off the Thames
from the British Airways Eye; and me, peering
intently, into Charles Dickens' bedside commode;
sunrise at Stonehenge, sundown at Tintern
with cows; gone, me, on the beach, listening
intently to that long withdrawing roar.—
Beneath a seat, industrial gray, halfway back
on the gritty floor in darkness, harbored now
past midnight, on some City-Sight-Seeing,
HopOn-HopOff, Stratford-Upon-Avon
red doubledecker, in the parking lot of the Pen
and Parchment Inn; on the lam; neatly nestled there.

Change

It came upon me that I might change, might wander
off down in valleys, where women gave suck
in the doorways, and deer and dark things hung
from oaks that swung in the wind. I saw I might
sway with the sound of gravel-on-tin the rain beat
the mountain with—so on I came, while the sky,
the sky was clogged with the colors of tattered fur.

Where were they, their rough coats, those battle-torn
banners proclaiming the sun? No one answered,
and no one came to explain from where or what tangle
of roots roared this storm in a bed in my little room,
this cackling here in the shadows, this loud dog set loose
in the lecture hall making me believe I might change.

Variations on a Theme by Ammons and Li Po

Last night on the National Geographic Channel
I watched an hour-long program
about the mountains of Hawaii. Bright green
in the extreme, and all the way to the top—
lime snow cone syrup, that green,
or like deep expensive jade along the base
and up among the cliffs
and the sharp, ridge-like peaks—
small trees and ferns
and a fecund moss that covers everything.

Jade Mountain then call it, this place
where I dwell. My house is halfway up
and on the west side. And when the sun
is overhead, the white butterflies sprinkle
themselves on my porch, assailing
the wild orchids' pink blossoms,
besotted in that rich foray.

Although the buttresses are steep, the climb
perhaps fatiguing and, well,
even perilous in places,
you would be welcome on Jade Mountain.
When I first came here
I brought with me a blender—
and I have put aside
ample Jose Cuervo
and margarita mix to stand the tests of Time.
And in the late afternoons, when the sun

dips down to mix with the Pacific,
I sit on my porch in quiet.

If you could manage to make it here by then,
we could share the quiet.
And I feel you would find the margaritas refreshing.
There is a brief period then
as the sky, which was white,
and the clouds, which were azure and gray,
glow orange and vermilion—
and the ocean, way down,
mirrors back all that
shimmering gold
as far as an eye can see.

O, come and breathe this propitious quiet.
You will find Jade Mountain sustaining.
There is much to be discussed,
but I think, perhaps, on some other occasion,
about the flutter of butterflies,
and how the horizon's magenta bleeds to the sea.
Much to be said, at a later date,
about the wondrous tang
of limes on the tongue—
this sunset worthy
of gracious remark.

And then the moon.

Listening to My Mother's Comic Banter with Sackboys and Servers

It is in brief moments such as these
that I know there is no God.
And I do not suppose that,
in even one of her eighty-
some-odd years, it has entered
my mother's mind that the look
in this young man's eyes, adrift
somewhere between shock and shame,
might ever be anything except
kindred and reciprocal laughter.
In his attempts at ascertaining
her desire to supersize her fries
or seeing her apples and Oreos
safely stowed, the server seems
caught off guard, and vaguely amazed
by my mother's grins and gab.
She, however, sees only a co-
conspirator, one who also gets
the joke with no name, her palaver
often beginning with something
along the lines of "working hard,"
then straight to "hardly working." Then,
if she perceives what she conceives
to be consent, the proper glance
or repartee, silence giving consent,
it eggs her on to escalate to snickers,
then, perhaps, to "Lord, it's hot! I'm

just a-sweatin'!" Graduating quick
enough from there to comments
maybe on the constant rise in
costs of things: "Shit fire to save
matches!" and beyond. Now, I
have borne witness to this bizarre
ascension many times. And always
at its end, I observe my mother's eyes
shifting from her daily dull to a fine
acetylene shine: opaque proof, at
best, of linkage to some living
thing outside herself. For
long ago I think somehow
my mother must have caught
a glimpse of some immense
and empty aught, some vacant
maw. And although she never
said so, would not even know
how to say so, it seems that,
ever since that time, she reaches
out to any sign, relying even on
the fantasized response of this
poor teenaged boy, as some bleak
buffer piled against confronting
that sad chasm once again, any
line to keep that zap of night
at bay, depending on any bray
of mindless blather, his requesting
now her preference for paper
over plastic, lilt, any semblance
of communion, the kindness
of strangers on any blessèd day.

Into the Furthest Regions

The enough is the largest land animal
—freshman essay

We managed to hire some indigenous
to carry our assorteds, and so trekked forward
through the doleful, overhanging verdurous
for many a slow prolong.
Then, suddenly, we broke out
onto the grassy everlasting.
Bright that shined, with a snow-capped immense
distant and ever away.
Still, no indicative,
but on the third revolving,
perceived it was at last, clifflike and wrinkled, and gray,
just standing there
sufficient, adequate, satisfactory—
surrounded by five spotted awkwards
and eight psoriatics,
and all these beneath
ravenous fecals circling in the blue.

Staple Song

Long queue the color of
concrete—tight column
strained with that ache
of anticipation traveling
down an Achilles tendon,
this formal life stretched
out along a taut, gray line,
lived always at attention,
caught at the bare brink
of the still stop of action,
are we not little soldiers,
stiff upper lips, each wait-
ing, dwelling in a starless
stasis,mon semblable,mon
frère? Oh, is this not the
essence of the urbanesque:
to stand in an unending
expectation, hungering—
for that piercing moment
when motion becomes
meaning, identical peas in
a dark pod, locked here
in this long, gray line?

Prelapsarian Dog Days on Lindell Avenue: 1972

Late one hot night
    Ralph called me into
        his room—long
    past midnight—
and we watched about
    a half-dozen mice,
        all sitting up
    on their haunches
around an upside-down
    mustard jar lid over
        in a shadowy corner.
    The only lights were
the guttering candles
    Ralph lit each evening
        to write his poems
    by; and the mustard
jar lid was filled with
    beige oats, a purchased
        poison which,
    Ralph explained, was
supposed to cause death
    within 24 hours
        by hotwiring
    the animal nervous system.
The oats must have been
    tasty indeed, because
        each avid mouse,
    oblivious to us, kept

stuffing itself with
    its own demise,
        those little cheeks
    puffed out like
Dizzy Gillespie's, but
    walnut-sized; and each
        of the mice sat
    holding even more death
in its tiny paws, waiting
    to cram that in too.
        It was the cutest thing
    I had seen that year,
and quite effective, for
    the very next morning,
        early was I roused
    by squeaks in the walls
and a disturbed rodent
    dying in my hair. Its death
        throes were violent
    and it fell to the floor
when I sat up. Shocked,
    surprised, I stopped
        its maniacal
    writhing by grabbing
one of the many anthologies
    I kept piled around
        my mattress back
    then (*The Contemporary
American Poets: American
    Poetry Since 1940*, ed.
        Mark Strand)
    and smashing that
elfin rat flat as any tortilla.

That Time of Year

He could sense it deep,
running through the October
leaf snows just beginning
then to drift down. Colors
of blood were the maple
leaves. But see, it was like
the last pickle in the jar
when your fork is too
short: swimming around,
bobbing away out of reach.
And it was the same when
he walked the gray beach.
Rough at the shore roared
the thick sea, but this faint
chattering of monkeys,
herds of monkeys behind
the sand dunes somewhere,
was always not there when
he went to see. He just
could not get at it, though
he often tried. At night
the usual stars flicked on,
leaving long, black rifts
filling most of the sky.
He studied, studied, but
he never could read what

the wind was saying when
it came muttering through
the many-taloned trees,
sifting far down through
the leaves such a thin sound
of fierce and senseless surgery.

Midway

That last night of the Southeast Texas State Fair,
your father refused to go inside
to see the freaks, but waited
outside the sideshow tent while you
wandered in alone to be amazed
by Abdulla, the Assyrian Sword Swallower,
and then by The 900 Pound Man,
and then by Melvin, the Mule-Faced Boy.

But when the time came for the grand finale,
the star attraction,
The Three-legged Man With Four Feet,
some guy came over and grabbed
your arm; said
the show was over; dragged you
to the exit and pushed you back outside.

In tears, you told your father, and he,
provoked, aroused, incensed and staunch
defender, took you over to the ticket seller
and demanded they let you back in.

Back on the front row, you beheld
the three-legged man shuffle out on stage
trailing clouds of glory,
sit down and begin to explain
the natural nature of things.
He wore a gray special-made suit
with an extra-wide third pants leg,
and then, when he pulled that pants leg up,

dangling worthlessly out, and seemingly
joined to the base of his spine,
was the thinnest third leg in the world,
him wriggling its toes to reveal
just how real.

Amid much applause
he pulled the pants leg up further, up
over his knee, and then—
the entire tent went still.

Coming out of his knee
where the kneecap should be
hung the fourth foot,
six inches long, worm-like
and white, hairless
and limp, with a hole at its end.

Outside again, the thick sweet reek
of old hamburger grease floated on the air.
And across the midway,
the nonstop barker of the *Totally Nude Review*
had ceased his babble and blab.
There, at the edge of night,
uncostumed men in denim
disassembled the Tilt-A-Whirl,
while a web of wrist-thick electric cables
crisscrossed the ground everywhere.

How quiet it seemed then.
Even today, you can still remember
how nothing was making a sound.
And when you looked up, you still
can recall, you saw no stars in the sky.

The Composition of *"The Eve of St. Agnes"* Followed in Late April by *"La Belle Dame Sans Merci"*

Coooeee. Mama says what's the point. I guess
she has been to town lots longer, like she says,
but I don't know. He seems so sweet sometimes.
He asked me over yesterday, a sunny day,
and Lord—even a bit on the warm side
for a change. So we went out back, behind
Mr. Brown's garden, to that plot of high grass
Mr. Brown says he plans to turn under
next month, so he can cultivate some corn.
Mr. Dilke says he will give that credence
when it's done. Now, Johnny brought this basket
filled with a half loaf and some white cheese,
and a little jar of brown beer as well.
—When we sat down in the grass I could tell
it was so we could be alone, the grass
being a bit higher than our heads. And sure
that was fine. Then he pulls a roll of papers
tied up with red ribbon from inside his coat,
and he says he has something for me.
Oh, do you? I say. He asks me do I know
the story of St. Agnes' Eve, and I say
no—for I could see he longed to tell it.
Of course, every girl learns such stuffings
at mother's knee, but I say mum's the word,
ha-ha. So, he unties the ribbons, and there
is his new poem, on the nicest paper,
all copied out neat in ink in his own hand.

He said the idea came upon him late January
when he and Mr. Brown were down to Chichester
and it had been so cold. He had been fiddling
with it ever since, nearly two months now.
He called me his pretty twin, like he does,
for when we walk people say we look alike,
our heights tracing out near about the same.
To tell it true, when I wear my hard heels
I stand a bit taller I think—I never before
being with a boy not higher than myself.
But that's nothing. He told me he has been
working on the poem in his bedroom, late
at night, until his eyes would sometimes get
all swimmy-like and blurry because of him
having just the two or three candles, and so
would have to stop till morning. He said
he loved that *his* bedroom now had been
my bedroom only last year, just seven months
before, until we moved over to Elm Cottage;
and he said at night he was sure my spirit
still lingered there. Well, I could see the drift
where we were headed clear as rain.—
Then he read his poem. Oh so finely done,
it seemed to me. I never learned so much
about poetry, or I guess almost anything—
but it looked lovely copied out like that
and sounded lovely too. As lovely maybe
as *Childe Harold*, I said. But that made him
make a funny face. I did not quite catch
each bit of it. There were some things going on
that sailed above me, but, coo, I heard
the part about the boy hiding in the closet
to watch the girl drop off her clothes for bed

all right. I saw the drift and how they ran
away at the end. And when he finished reading
he looked up, and sure he had tears in his eyes,
so tender, flushed near like a pink rose.
—He rolled the papers back up, tied them tight
with the red ribbons, and handed them to me.
Then he reached over, just that soft, and took
my hand, and kissed me. And I let him.
Then, he touched me, you know, there.
But that's nothing. I let William do the same
last summer and why not? Such private things
between those who care seems fine—as right
as rain to me. He whispered my name, over
and over; then I of course said his name back.
We held each other close for what did seem
the longest time. And then we were quiet,
like people often get after such goings-on,
and picked up the picnic things and wandered
back to the house and Mr. Brown's parlour.
—Just last week, Mr. Dilke said he will make
a grand poet. And Mr. Brown says he is one.
I've heard others say the same, but Mama says
be careful. Mama says you can't eat poems
or wear them. She says the way things are
a woman had best fashion out each single step
before she takes it. And if you can't cock
a careful eye to the far side of a door—
you best not waltz on through until you can.
Well now, sure, there seems some smart,
I guess, in all of that.—But I don't know.

Room with a View

Higgledy-piggledy
Emily Dickinson
Looked out her front window
Struggling for breath—

Suffering slightly from
Agoraphobia:
"Think I'll just—stay in and—
Write about—Death—"

Roger O. Thornhill on Mount Rushmore

—North by Northwest

Hanging by one hand, from the stone coat lapel
of The Father of Our Country, hanging on
by that hand, and holding by the other, Eve,
the new beginning, all that's best of blonde
and bright, trying at long last not to assent
again to his initials' implications (R.O.T.),
and simultaneously having to contend with
Leonard, whose "woman's intuition," like his shoe,
is, at this moment, applying a painful pressure
to Roger O. Thornhill's tenuous fingerhold
on the permanence, the stability, made manifest
by this gigantic, granite rendering of the guy
who would not ever support the telling of a lie—
Roger begs for Leonard's aid, and we realize Roger
is requesting help from the wrong cabellero. But
then the LAW arrives! Leonard and his big shoe
fall away. Hitchcock, the Master, rarely sending
his patrons home deprived, makes his dark point,
then calculates just what the folks in Omaha
require, leaving Roger Thornhill free, despite
Eve's strong misgivings, her clear agitation
and naked fear, to lift her up to make it in his arms.

Colonel Kilgore's Complaint

"Someday this war's gonna end. . . ."
—Robert Duvall in *Apocalypse Now*

Coppola knew all temporal forms tell us
Time Marches On, like those black-and-white
newsreels from the forties. And he knew

the implications woven into what
is wrought along that temporal line;
but he felt it was his job to discover—

to lift up—the moment when the perceiver
might most fathom that relentless tide.
The moment, he believed, needs to be

near violence, but not within it, so the perceiver
might be aroused, might heed it there,
epiphanous, where it had not

been before. This is why Colonel Kilgore,
Robert Duvall, pauses, then looks out over
the horizon the way he does. The battle

is done: AIR CAV mopping up now, mostly. Then,
with the same care Hopkins uses explaining
autumn to a little girl, the morning

dripping cognac down through the grove's golden leaves,
Kilgore speaks. Relating an old war story
of remembered joy so strange

it is like lip-syncs from another world,
    barely audible against the din of carnage
        in the background, the occasional blasts

of mortar shells up and down the beach—
    he preludes the approaching *moment*
        with his lines about "the smell

of napalm in the morning," the smell
    of "victory,"— overtures upholding,
        like a colonnade, this tiny frieze

carved on the entablature of Time. Then,
    crouching down in his hunter's squat,
        and with a voice more worn than any other,

Kilgore glances up at Martin Sheen—
    his grimace ancient, antediluvian—and remarks,
        in his fashion, how all beauty must rot and wane.

The Gold Rush

"We make our meek adjustments."
—Hart Crane

Let us enter pursued by a bear.
        The balmy lord doffs
his derby. Snow swirls everywhere.
        Always the cold, always
the stumbling from place to small place

to shut out the meanings of snow
        for a while. Tied
to a dog that dragged him from grace,
        remember the night, that
New Year's Eve when he opened

his door and a mule walked in?
        Then we were the one,
the acquaintance forgot, the face
        of despair, tottering there on that
distant cliff. Snow swirls everywhere.

8½

In black and white, a little boy runs
down a beach pursued by priests.
Almost the young boy's earliest recalled desire
is to pee in the padre's chalice,
or to spit in the padre's pyx,
or sneak a drink
of Monsignor's best Chianti,
as acolytes are often wont to do. But no.

Soon enough, in black and white,
the little boy runs through a house
full of Mama and nurses and aunts.
Mama is bathing her little Guido,
swathing her lovely all in towels,
warm like swaddling, and ready
to be kissed and carried upstairs to bed. But no.

At last, the little boy runs down the beach
by himself, past salt marsh and sea grass,
the sea breeze flapping his black Catholic cape
as he comes up short, then stares
at "La Saraghina,"
the mascaraed mountain
of greasepaint, udders and leers,
sitting alone in her chair
on the beach, gazing forlornly out to sea.

The little boy holds out coins in his hands,
offers her lire to dance the rumba
while he sits and watches,
dance the rumba
while he sits and stares.
And O, she smiles
as he ponders her rise—
smiles while he watches
those enormous haunches
sway in the sea sand.
Caught in that cadence
and stamp, he stares:
berouged Saraghina,
calloused heels
stomping her ictus
on sea sand,
bare feet pounding
her rhythm on the shore.

You Are Here

Twenty bucks for the Wakulla Springs
Covered Boat Jungle Cruise, to see
"The Alligator in His Natural Habitat"
and "The Actual Site
of the On-Location Filming
of *The Creature from the Black Lagoon*"
seemed a real deal to my wife and me.

Except that the guide
of the Covered Boat Jungle Cruise
kept repeating into his microphone:
Now up here on ya right
ya got your gator.
That one there
bein Oh
about
eighty year old,
by my recknin.
Now up here on ya left—

And, by my count, five
separate times saying:
—Now up here on ya left
ya got your anhinga—
                                        Fabled fowl!
Snakebird or water turkey!
Anhinga!
Gotta sit and spread them wings to dry—
before he can fly!

And the mother on the bench behind us:
Cissy. Be careful. Cissy.
Cissy. Leave
the man's hair alone, Cissy.
Cissy!
Now aren't you ashamed!

Deep, dark green water.
Frayed beards of Spanish moss
hanging from the cypress trees.
An osprey floating through a crystal sky.
And the anhinga,
"... Fabled fowl!
Snakebird or water turkey!"
He must sit still just a little longer
before he can fly away.

The Point Envenom'd Too!

From the second balcony
the prince was a black stumbling ant
or mote swirled in white footlights
or perhaps any asking and quick
indistinguishable thing—
very like a quail flapping fast
out in front of your car spilling
from its mouth small sounds

Watching My Mother Take Her Last Breath

People ground down by what the doctors call
"acute COPD" have not much but a vacuum
left inside when the ache of that last onset
invades the hospice air. But even though
that's so, and even though there came a time
when what she wanted most was just to sail
away, the body holds some tenets of its own.
There, at the end, I saw my mother's mouth
become a perfect round, a ring, a dark hole
clearly larger than it ever seemed before—
and it strove, I thought, through the scrim
of morphine, to draw into that dim chasm
everything it could. O, let the earth be
shoveled in, it seemed to say. O, let now be
consumed into this disk of dark, this gape,
the air and every small or massive entity—
all this lonely, frightened, wanting, weary,
sad and hurting woman has throughout
her little and long life never known. And then,
the heaving ceased. And the great shroud of the sea
rolled on as it rolled five thousand years ago.

Burnt Bridges

Like an old Ethel Waters 78 of "Stormy Weather,"
white trash, indigents, drunks, and thieves
cried out in the streets all night. And when I
woke, to rat-infested walls and water stains
like Rorschachs on the ceiling, I still could
hear them scream. The wars against gravity
would not be won there, I could tell. And so
I left, and as I left I once again burnt bridges.

Hard winds and endless rain brought many down.
This wind is cold. It pricks and stings. It singes
the skin of me, the man of mode, impervious to
irony. I shrug, shake, then wrap this habit round.
How oddly exquisite the far horizon seems.

Legacy

for Erin

Just so, when they come demanding,
you might possess some grasp of facts—
just in case motivations at some point
might appear unclear—just
to insure with certainty

you will recall later on: take
one peeled cucumber and grate it
finely as you can. Swirl this and the juice
of two lemons in one pint
of yogurt, setting it

aside somewhere, cold. So
there will remain some record, cube
three pounds of lamb, then sauté it
lightly floured, in a skillet
with one stick of butter, dice

one large onion, then combine
the meat and onion in a stew pot
under water to drown it all. To this
mixture add three bay leaves, add
three cloves of garlic

crushed. Add one tablespoon
of pepper, then one tablespoon of salt. In-
to that you sprinkle cumin: two
tablespoons, and then to make it
strange, three heaping

teaspoonfuls of powdered
cardamom, a grayish beige in its dry
state (but it will turn the water green),
and then you cover this and cook it
for three hours on low heat: stir

the stew occasionally, but
do not let the juices boil away. Remember:
when they come in the night, screaming,
with their torches, beseeching
you, fingers of torchlight

warping their wan faces
in the dark, your front porch flickering
unearthly, remember then what
I say now: after the lamb
has simmered for three hours,

in a separate saucepan
cook two cups of rice. While the rice
is cooking, peel, then slice into white
inch-thick circles, three large
eggplants. Fry each

slice in peanut oil
in a skillet until browned; then place
the eggplant out on paper towels
to soak some oil away—
(by now the cardamom

has drenched your house
in incense: massive hints of orient
and odalisque, Babylon and Berber,
Bedouin and myrrh). Just
so I will know you

know, layer in a casserole
first the lamb, then the eggplant, then
rice on top of that: lamb again, egg-
plant, rice, until the dish
is almost full—then

pour the chartreuse
liquor on it: bake it covered
for an hour, in an oven at three hundred
eighty-five degrees—but whatever
else, do not forget

they will be coming, certain
as the glacier's pain, wrapped in cowls,
in their injunctions, screws and ropes,
racks and chains, insisting
you confess

your sickness, producing writs
commanding you disclose what sources
taught you to concoct such venom,
declaring all your actions
darkness, everything you live for

bane. Child, do not answer,
do not listen. Deny them. Lie to them
at every path (a thick, green, good,
sweet pungency for hours
will have lacquered

every wall, satiated, smeared
the air, redolent, ancient, with a tang
of loam or salt or sea) but remember
when the dish comes from the oven
you must serve it

right away. In the middle
of a large, hot, black plate, stack
a steaming mountain of the lamb—
then along its peak, pile
three dollops of the yogurt

blend—late spring snows
melting from the sun, cascading off
the mountainside in milky tributaries,
tiny runny rivulets winding
down then out to sea. And

at this point in time, when
the heat and cold conjoin, you must
call forth your belovèd. You must sit
your belovèd down. You must ask
of your belovèd

if there is need of any thing,
placing upon the table, then, this plate
you have prepared, permitting this creation
(Know they will be coming! They
carry oaken rams to batter

in your door!) to be consumed,
daughter, and when your dish is tasted—
O, at that precise moment, daughter,
from all previous moorings
the heart will be set free.

Georgia Gothic

Lafayette, Ga.—At the end of a 10-hour court day packed with emotions alternating from rage to sadness, Tri-State Crematory operator Ray Brent Marsh was sentenced to 12 years in prison, in accordance with a negotiated agreement with prosecutors. At the official allocution, Marsh was asked why . . .

—Atlanta Journal-Constitution

Not that long ago, in a country
    not that far away, there lived
a crematorium owner/operator
whose mind was often elsewhere.
                    Some mornings,
he might rise, and view himself
    in the mirror, and think,
"My head feels all drifted
    and bent astray."
                    Then,
    he would wander down
to the brambled woods
    behind his business
for an hour's aimless saunter.

                    Who knows
what thoughts compelled him
    on his forest rambles—
but one April afternoon
    he returned to find
        his crematorium oven
    would not function right.
It would not heat up
    high enough to blaze

even the minor bones away.
    And although he found
        the part he needed
in *Cremation Monthly*—
    had money enough
    to purchase it as well—
he never got around
    to making that call.

Instead, he thought hard
    at the desk in his tiny office
        about those two
    new bodies waiting
        to be inflamed—
then had a thought he
    had not thought before.

After dark, he bundled
    both in plastic sheets,
        carried them both
to the vacant shed out back,
    placed them gently
    in one corner, grabbed
a couple of pine logs, hauled
    those back to the oven,
        burned them
to ash, blended that ash
    with cement dust,
then divided the mix
    into the appropriate boxes,
        labeled them, then—
mailed each on its way.
And after that it was only

a matter of storage:
embalmed remains
not smelling terribly bad.

But four years later that shed
was filled to the top,
and the weathered,
dilapidated, unused
garage as well; so
he took to lugging
the bodies back in the woods,
then laying each beneath
some bush or tree.

Then came the day
the Dawkins boy slipped in.

Squirrel-hunting kids
pay no attention
to POSTED signs
and trespass where they please,
but what this boy saw
under low limbs
that autumn morn was enough
to give him pause, enough
to shake him, turn him,
fire him fast back home
to Daddy, his dog, his
sister's smile—anything unlike
dried nightmares under pines.

The law was called. Three
hundred thirty-four

bodies found stashed around
the workplace, many long
    past being identified.
        Over 400 felony counts
            of theft; 49 counts
of making false statements;
        plus 122 counts
            of burial service
fraud and 179 counts
    of abuse of a corpse.

    Twenty-five death threats.
No bail. The Walker
        County district attorney
asked him why. Why
        might he commit this
crime three hundred times?
To which the dazed
    owner/operator, Ray
        Brent Marsh, replied
            he meant to get
the oven fixed but—
    he guessed his mind
        was elsewhere. He
guessed, he said, it had
        drifted a bit astray.

To a Nightingale

Anonymous as elephant
dung trampled in the straw

of the menagerie beside
the Ringling Brothers

Barnum & Bailey
Circus tent, then

smeared on my new shoe
when I was four—

anonymous,
this unsigned envelope

in my department
mailbox I rip open

to reveal: **YOU**
ARE A BAd Poet

AND A FAT APple
in an array of fonts,

like a cut-out ransom
note aimed at retaliation.

Assertive assonance aside,
I know damned

well this sprang full-
formed from the bristled

brain of Mister Oglesby!
whose refusal

to revise, on principle,
refusal to amend

in any way, the unpre-
meditated pourings-

forth of his seeming
bird-song soul in such

an ecstasy, fanned
the forked and frothy

flames of friction
in recent class

discussions. Oh
Mister Oglesby!

This brief epistle here—
so unlike your odd,

obscurant and, no
doubt, hallucinogenic

scrawled ejaculations
dumped forth upon

some darkling plain
during the tender mid-

night of two days ago,
then trundled up

and hauled to class
on yestereve—

concerning this raw
missive, Señor

Oglesby!—destroyer
of worlds—allow

me to quick-cut
here to repartee—

Bird thou never wert!
nor will ever be—

and what artistic
excretions of le monde

you might have
dreamt exuding

from your so-called
mind are fled forever

through that rusty
back screen door,

retreating fast
down a twilit, bent,

and scraggly path
to dwell, submerged

out there somewhere,
buried now, deep

within the dried-up
innards of some

storm-swept,
gray

and splintered,
unremembered

shithouse.

These Days

These days I live on top of a piney ridge
outside Atlanta. And this November morning
at daybreak, I stepped out on the back patio
with my first cup of coffee and there it was:
that blood red sun creeping through a black
latticework of limbs, the few leaves left of pine
and oak. And where the woods slope down
to the creek, those trees are ninety feet high,
as big as they become in northern Georgia.
Then, when the sunlight filtered through,
to pour out on the pre-dawn mist, it turned
that low two feet of fog soft lavender. Then
I remembered I had seen this scene, though
changed somewhat, I think, somewhere before.

Back in 1965, my parents and I lived eight
miles north of the little Texas town of Silsbee;
and each weekday I would rise at 5, to be
picked up by 7, then carpooled thirty miles
to Beaumont, to attend the Lamar State College
of Technology. And while I waited for my ride,
I would step outside with my coffee cup
to watch the sun rise over the long pasture
on the east side of the clapboard company house
where my family stayed rent free—across
the road from the warehouse and pipe yard
my father ran for Sinclair Oil and Gas.

And when the light burst through the forest
at the far end of Weaver's well-cropped field,

then struck that low mist and the dew—
it took my breath away. It took my breath
away—because I never in my life had seen
a sight so very fine, so beautiful, so new.
And it was the same view, the same view then
as now: the same red rubber ball impaled upon
the same dark spires of pines. The same light
amethyst or orchid counterpane of vapors
there beneath my feet. No change at all.
What changed, it dawned today, was a feeling,
missing here, that *was* back then. A bloom,
a bounce, the rich rush of fire that spread
through everything. And I thought that was
how life was bound to be. Not this strange
numbness, this lack in time—this pencil drawing
of the bright world gone, which leaves you
looking down the longest hall, tense,
and drifting toward—regardless of what
you do, or want to do, or say—a permanent
pause—preceded only by the ever constant sense
of an engine grinding down. That takes my breath away.

Even Now

There have been times when the blood within
has ached with the thunder of horses,
has been like the din of a thousand horses' hooves—

and still I can hear them pounding,
even now, when my mind is calm, the hooves of horses,
still filling my ears with their sound—

and the long rippling flanks are like pistons,
the rhythm of speed and of sweat—
always the hunger of horses,

always the clamor and roar,
of my death I want only horses—
in my memory, nothing before.

II ✷ AUTUMN RHYTHM (1996)

He supposed this was what life taught you,
that words you thought were a joke,
and applied to someone else,
were real, and applied to you.

—Louis Simpson

Evening's End

1943–1970

For the first time in what must be
the better part of two years now
I happened to hear Janis
in her glory—
all that tinctured syrup
dripping off
a razorblade—
on the radio today singing "Summertime."

And it took me back to this girl I knew,
a woman really, my first year
writing undergraduate poetry
at the Mirabeau B. Lamar
State College of Technology
in Beaumont, Texas,
back in 1966.

This woman was the latest in a line,
the latest steady
of my friend John Coyle that spring—
and I remember she was plain:
she was short: and plain
and wore her brown hair up
in a sort of bun in back
that made her plainer still.

I don't know where John met her,
but word went round

she had moved back in with Mom and Dad
down in Port Arthur
to get her head straight,
to attend Lamar,
to study History,
after several years in San Francisco
where she had drifted
into a "bad scene"
taking heroin.

I was twenty,
still lived with Mom and Dad myself,
and so knew nothing
about "bad scenes,"
but I do remember once or twice
each month that spring
John would give a party
with this woman always there.
And always as the evening's end came on
this woman, silent for hours,
would reveal, from thin air,
her guitar,
settle in a chair,
release her long hair
from the bun it was in,
and begin.

Her hair flowed over her shoulders,
and the ends of the strands of hair
like tarnished brass in lamplight
would brush and drag across

the sides of the guitar
as this woman bent
over it.

How low and guttural, how
slow and torchlit, how
amber her song, how absolutely
unlike the tiny nondescript
a few minutes before.—

And I remember also,
from later on that spring,
from May of that year,
two nights in particular.

The first night was a party
this woman gave
at her parents' home.
Her parents' home
was beige:
the bricks the parents' home
was built with
were beige.
The entire house was carpeted
in beige.

John's girl greeted everyone at the door,
a martini in one hand
and a lit cigarette
in an Oriental
ivory cigarette holder in the other,

laughing
for once, and tossing back
her long brown hair.

All the women wore
black full-length party dresses—
and I remember the young woman's father,
how odd he seemed
in his charcoal suit and tie,
his gray hair—
how unamused.

Then John Coyle was drunk.
He spilled his beer
across the beige front room carpet:
that darker dampness sinking in,
the father vanished
from the scene.

The next week we double-dated.
I convinced John and his girl
to see a double feature,
Irma La Douce and Tom Jones,
at the Pines Theatre.
And I can recall John's girl
saying just one thing that night.

After the films, John was quizzical,
contentious, full of ridicule
for movies I had guaranteed he would enjoy.
He turned and asked her
what she thought—
and in the softest

of tones, a vague rumor
of honeysuckle in the air,
she almost whispered,
"I thought they were beautiful."

That was the last time that I saw her,
the last thing that I heard her say.

A few weeks later,
she drove over to John's house
in the middle of the afternoon,
and caught him in bed
with Suzanne Morain,
a graduate assistant
from the English Department at Lamar.

John told me later
that when she saw them in the bedroom
she ran into the kitchen,
picked up a broom,
and began to sweep the floor—
weeping.

When John sauntered in
she threw the broom at him,
ran out the door,
got in her car and drove away.
And from that day on,
no one ever saw that woman
in Beaumont again.

The next day she moved to Austin.
And later on, I heard,

back to San Francisco.
And I remember when John told me this,
with a semi-shocked expression
on his face, he turned
and looked up, and said, "You know,
I guess she must have really *loved* me."

I was twenty years old.
What did I know?
What could I say?

I could not think
of anything to say,
except, "Yes,
I guess so."

It was summertime.

Thus runs the world away.

The Garden Path

When my bloodshot eyes
grow tired from reading
all day long, why I just
look how no child comes
down the garden path
with a leaf of grass
and questions; and if
one did, "On the fringes
always, on the fringes,"
I might say. But how
to explain this need
of us and three black
grizzlies skating on ice
drunk, mad to break through
down where waters run? I
could say that, or say
as in other things
only skin deep we get
to go. There's blood
down there, blankness, I
could say if some child
came, we'd see the last
shaft of sun those miners
ever saw there, naked,
thoughts of men who leap
from ledges, "You knew
Sanders died." "No."
as sad soldiers fall
from horses and lie
frozen in the snow.

The Royal Nonesuch

Extempore Effusion upon the Death of Everette Maddox (1944–1989)

Given recent events,
it's easy to see why
that bilgewater-slick
New Orleans night
stink stays stuck
in the craw. Almost
midnight in The Maple
Leaf, and you, Big E.,
querulous for hours,
while black cascades
of rain made mighty sure
the never-ending steam-
bath just kept roaring.
Across Oak Street, through
the front bar window,
the red and blue *KINKO'S*
flickered and
flashed, reflecting
in the street like rubies
and sapphires. Then up
through the mildew, up
through the smoke, up off
that sticky Dixie Beer
floor, you raised it
at last, dog-eared
and dirty, on high
for me to read. And

I was so smitten, so
enamored, by
the incredible original
aptness of the title
of that somewhat-soiled
manuscript version
of your 2nd collection,
I exclaimed, "Damn!
I'll swap you one
fifth of Chivas for
the use of this!" And,
to my surprise, you
whispered, "OK." Given
recent events, I wish
I had offered a big
beef filet. But even
back then, you were, by
far, the absolutely
thinnest person I
had seen: only man
to match poem and
body to perfection:
paring things down
to the barest bone.
Given recent events,
and in verification
of your claim
that black steam-
bath night back
in 1983, something
a bit like sapphires
and rubies gleaming
in the streets, and

with, perhaps, just
a touch of a hint
of intent toward late
reparations, let me
say, sad pal, skinny
feller, funny friend,
and as the record runs
down now, you are, no
doubt about it, and
irrevocably so,
the one and the only,
the late Dauphin.

Bottom's Dream

Methought I was—there is no man can tell what
—A Midsummer Night's Dream

I'm the kind of guy who finds himself past midnight
halfway down the frigging kudzu-covered
woodbine-shaded moonlit emblematic forest path
self-conscious to a fault and wondering what
the hell these numerous assorted dead ends
are supposed to tally up to anyway.
"Jesus,
Jesus, Jesus," I have upon occasion in the dark
remarked, but don't think, by your leave,
I ever hung around expecting some response
to such direct address.
No.
I may be just the country cousin
forced sometime to city fair
to make a buck and to try my luck,
to tote and grunt, to cart
my baggage, hoist
my wares—my mildewed merchandise,
such as it is and so to speak—
but I ain't that dumb.
No
mother's son ever had to explain to me
that we are the zapped, the oblivion riders,
totally lacking—from the first time
that we mewl and cry—even a Chinaman's chance

of knowing the soiled shorts of a sick shyster
from a sack of sugar about the least damned thing.

Observe this bird, that bear, the wild herbs flowing down
yon fecund bank in damp and pearly moonshine.
As they are, so are we: tiny pitiful cogs
which scrape and grind the stars across the sky each night
only for all to dissolve at dawn.
                                        And yet,
come morning I am still possessed by these brief
scenes, mists, vapors, frenzied residues.
                                                  But residues
of what? If man is but a bird, a bush, a bank
where the wild thyme blows; if, as to variations,
'tis all one between the ploughman, who comes and turns
the earth then lies beneath, and this bear
besmirching his face tonight with berries
only to besmear tomorrow his own buttocks with the same;
if all fall down in the great schemata,
why am I then left with these bad shreds of dreams,
these scraps of hair and hay,
these cobweb patches?
If I could get my hands back down beneath
the muck and stew, back down beneath
these floating fumes—
but such abiding wraiths, such furtive lingerers,
will not disperse. And all attempts become attempts
toward fathoming the unfathomable. Why
how exceedingly erectus, how very
pithecanthropine of me!

Swirling indistinct chimeras, I see them there
drifting up out of their own miasmal goo, from how

far down I think I'll never know, but if I perhaps
could offer to imbue them with the vestments
of this same locale—the vestments, say,
that I might wear me of a summer's day—
might they not then choose
to turn and to expound, having taken on
the accoutrements of said habitat, taking on
its language and its names as well?

And might we then converse us, our same raiments
engendering a commerce that we each could comprehend?
Or would these reveries, like great festering palms
swaying in their orchid fog, despite whatever garb
I might conceive, fold back into the dark quintessence
from which they came, continuing, forever, to exude
only the exotic, the entirely other, the secret idiom
lost in translation, distant, dim, inscrutable still?

Reynaldo in Paris

"Ooo-la-la!" remarked Reynaldo. "Tonight
my wick shall dip in ecstasies once more
as I plunge deeper through that nunnery door,
Miss Mimi's house of sale, then jam it tight.
Back home, I smelled the rotten fault all right,
so took the bucks and split from that dumb bore
and got out while the gettin' was good, before
shit hit the fan and blotted out the light.

What wine so sweet as little Mimi's seat!
Now that's the song I'm singing every day.
So let them grab each other by the balls.
For what care I whose slick, incestuous meat
gets gnawed between those sheets. And, what care they
for fardel-bearing sots who play their thralls."

Jaques Lured by Audrey

As the ox hath his bow

—As You Like It

I swear I know not how, but as fleeting as
ice sculptures melting on a summer lawn,
opalescent in moonlight, winking like dark jade
out on the damp grass and away, these globes
of memory dissolve right down into the earth
as quick as all these goat droppings will in rain.
This very forest floor must be engorged by now
with generations of droppings, but no one sees
or cares. And how it happened I do not know, but
since that brief merger, since we pleasures proved,
O my adult arcade, my nut-brown study, my sylvan
nocturne in burnished beige and gold, it has been
like knocking at the deaf man's door of my brain
to thrust anything through there but that one moment,
this stopped dot of you growing more obscure each day,
your goat-reek rank on my hands like fresh garlic
and mint from the garden. How banish this dot
of you! Even though the thought itself is black
ink turning brown, this want will not burn down.
It flares in here, a never-flickering auto-da-fé,
an urge that will not purge, forever a hunger
nearly gnawing its way out. Banished now from
my own being, swaddled all in motley now, my
only wear—might we, together, be that beast
again, crushed mint, garlic, reek, balm, that ram,
O my tiny Temptation of Saint Anthony, together
might we make once more our common, curful cry.

An Inkling

Just two weeks graduated from Central High
in 1942, my mother finds herself
employed as the candy girl
at the State Theatre
in downtown Oklahoma City. And just
across the street, at the Liberty Theatre,
my father, who does not know
my mother yet, is head usher,
although Assistant Manager
is his actual title,
as he is quick to tell.

From where she stands, my mother
sometimes gazes across the street
and sees my father taking tickets,
sweeping, changing the marquee.

He really is a pretty boy,
she thinks. And she
is not alone. All the usherettes
at the State think so too.
And they have all, all that are
in the game anyway, given him
a shot, a little wiggle, the once-over,
the come-on, these last few weeks,
to no avail. Why is that?
My mother does not know.

There is a war on, and there
are Army and Navy boys

everywhere, half of them not much
or no older than herself,
but god, doesn't he look divine
in that navy-blue head usher's uniform,
with gold braid up and down
each arm and pants leg too,
and gold buttons, and epaulets
with gold fringe hanging off.

She thinks how fine they both
might look together on a date,
but her State uniform
is green, pool-table-green,
with dark green braid
and buttons too. Even so,
she loves it. The pants
and jacket make her think
of Dr. Dolittle. She remembers
reading Dr. Dolittle back
ten years before. Her favorite book
had been *Dr. Dolittle and the Secret Lake*
because it was so thick.
It made her blush
when people came up
and remarked how smart
she must be to read
such a big book.
So she read it four times.

But she remembers also
the picture on the cover
with Dr. Dolittle in his pooltable-
green jacket and trousers,
or were they called pantaloons?

She cannot recall.
And then, one week later,
Charlene is out front, and she says
something to my father, and he says
something back, and he smiles.
And when my mother,
from behind the candy counter
and the tinted plate-glass doors,
sees that smile,
that settles things.

Something in that smile. So
by mid-July she has dropped
her crumbs, she has stood
upwind, she has cast her line,
and he has bit the bait, her hook
now nestled tight against
the inside of his lower lip,
and she is seriously
considering hauling him in.

On their third date he borrows a car,
and after work they go
to Beverly's Drive-In and order
Chicken-in-the-Rough. She spent
weekends and holidays the year before
as a carhop there: Beverly's
is perfect. Beverly's is A-OK.
Beverly's is divine.

Then she shows him a place
out by Indian Stadium
where they can park

and spend some time alone.
They have not worn
their uniforms, and she is glad
she had not asked him to. They stop
at the far end of the stadium
parking lot. The moonlight
shining on the gravel gray
has turned it the color of mercury.
My father turns, and puts his arm
around my mother, and kisses her,
and then he looks down,
and lifts his other hand,
and rests it gently, Oh
so gently, against my mother's
blouse.
            He then applies
a small amount of pressure.
He wants her to see that
he is kind, but firm. And so,
gently, he applies pressure
to her blouse, and thus
to the bra beneath that blouse,
and, thus, to the breast
beneath that bra. And he looks down
into her eyes, questioning. Hesitant,
but firm.
            And my mother looks
up into the glow and darkness
and sees that question there.
An omen, maybe. An inkling.
And it makes her think, for just
an instant, of her own father, Clyde,
four years back. Clyde had never

questioned, had he? Oh no.
That bourbon-breath on top of her,
that ape-like pawing,
pushing her down, the reek
and stink of whiskey over
everything, and the stumbling off
afterward, off her bed and out
into the kitchen to vomit and pass out
like the pig he was. The next day,
her mama took her on the bus
eighty-five miles from Weatherford
to Oklahoma City and the good
open arms and home of Aunt Helen.
But then her mama rode right back
to Weatherford and stayed.
For more than one whole year
she stayed—until Clyde beat
her up and ran off one last time.

So my mother lifts her eyes
and sees that questioning. She notices,
too, a tiny band of platinum—
perspiration—above my father's lip,
for, although it is past midnight,
it stays hot in Oklahoma City
in the summertime. In ten months
my father will be sweating more
with a fever of one hundred and five,
having contracted malaria
on the island of New Guinea,
soon to be sent stateside
as his only cure. But now my mother
gazes up at my father's eyes.

I tell you she looks up,
and she sees what is in
my father's eyes, and what
will be in my father's eyes,
and what will never be
in my father's eyes, this once
and future moralist wanting
always to do good, to strive,
to find. This pretty boy.

She drops her gaze again
to see the moon's milk spilt
all down the front of her blouse,
and all over my father's hand
resting, firmly, there.
Then she rests her own hand
on the steering wheel, shifts
slightly, and leans her heavy head
against my father's shoulder.
As she does so, she can feel
the taut muscles along the back
of her neck begin to ease.

She shivers for a second,
then meets his eyes, those obscure
agents of augury, once more.
He is smiling. Such
a gentle face, with such
a gentle smile. And so
she smiles back at him.
And it is in this fashion,
with all the world at war,
that my mother smiles back,

to let my father know that
this will do. This is
satisfactory. This little sphere
inside this Ford at one end
of this empty parking lot
will do for her, she seems
to say, as she glances down again,
with the whole world swirled
in shades of pearl and mercury,
at her breast laved in moonlight,
at my father's hand resting there,
questioning. And it is thus
that she cedes to him,
as though through a scrim
of reverie, that small concession.

Fall

One lit match and there they go.
Like a revolution.

To jump into that

would be death.

But we are all sane people here.
Here is where
we fight it off
with rakes.

We keep it at bay.

It would mean death.

So

soon,
only the white ash is left.

I Greet You

Higgledy-piggledy
Ralph Waldo Emerson
Often wrote poems that
Lay down and died.

Walt Whitman sent him his
Preponderatingly
Better book. Emerson
Read it, and cried.

Morte d'Arthur

Higgledy-piggledy
Alfred, Lord Tennyson
Lost his pal Hallam to
Fever and flu:

"One hundred thirty-one
Ultramemorial
Verses and, man, I still
Can't bury you."

Kitty Litter

Higgledy-piggledy
"Old Possom" Eliot
Wrote childish verse about
Practical cats.

"These are for all of you
Abecedarians,
Idiots, simpletons,
Moronic brats."

Homework

Higgledy-piggledy
Erin Elizabeth
Stokesbury said, "Math is
Too hard for me."

O for those summers of
Unalgebraical
13 + 2 –
12 – 3.

Pro Quo

Higgledy-piggledy
Sergei M. Eisenstein
Needed State financing:
Film is not free.

"Only," said Stalin, "if
Revisionistically
Ivan the Terrible
Acts just like me."

Dark Blurb of the Soul

". . . Seems to me to be
one of that breed who, when
he approaches Dallas from
the north, sees, welling
up, gold chunks of buildings,
great glass in the sun, row
over row of gold teeth, hog
grins, glistening, blind.
Here we have the mnemonic
daring, the nasty clarity,
the handprint of necessity
of one of those 'intellectuals'
attempting the flamenco
over a Big Abyss. This
is the kind of bore who views
the abominable Hawaiian
photo of Mom and Uncle
Joe, loud shirts, volcano
in the background, and then
lets the sad sow metaphors
multiply and cry. This is
he, this is he who sees
the burned girl, that fried
face's texture like plastic
puke, and aches to get his
hands on all that saffron
and blue. Reading this entity
is stepping off into

slime, into little fishes, fast
and crappy creatures nipping
at your knees. Subtleties
of rhythm? Subtleties of
rhyme? If swine had wings,
this guy would fly . . ."

Señor Wences and the Man in the Box

L. B. Stokesbury (1924–1987)

Jokester, prankster, petty gangster, son,
let me see you laugh your way out of this one.
No one should know better than you
except maybe now me, that there is no word, no posy,
no black scratch on the white eyeball of blankness,
no pisshole in snow, that can capture
for even an instant
what anyone really is at any time. And so,
and even so, laddybuck, my little Sisyphus,
prankster, son, I lie here now
blessed to watch your scared frown staring down.

And what did you expect? Some hideous
blaming rictus glaring back? What you deserved
for the thousand times you flashed
that crappy gaze of yours
that said I owed you something
obligatory, a gift I never gave? Oh
no. Not me. And not here, assuredly. No.

But if I do owe you something, if there is
a remembrance that you might in faith require,
some faint sachet to hold before the nose in future years,
maybe this will do:
last night, myself sequestered here,
my cheeks having taken on a certain pale,
no longer imbued

with their usual natural cutaneous hue
but with white rather,
ash white, whale
white, lead white, dare I say
dead white, while I was just
lying here extremely still, cold toes
saluting the North Star,
a pimply boy I never in my life had seen before
stepped softly up and violently
massaged the muscles of my cheek and jaw.
Then he jammed a piece of plastic,
a sort of warped elongated
MasterCard, in each corner of my mouth
between the lip and gum. Then
with a slick, quick, solid push and pull
he popped the plastic out, leaving
this look I lie here with today:
this look you are staring at right now:
a look they label as *serene*.

How's that? OK? You can have it.
On the house. A nosegay.

Ah, laddybuck, if we could have found
some demilitarized zone, which we could not;
if I could for once
have raised you up out of your maze of corridors,
which I could not; you
with your boxcars of words words words:
little links of ink lined up all in a row, chugging

off toward the horizon; maybe then
I could have told you what you wanted to hear.

Instead, only this:
myself, disassembling, desirous to consign
my pressing embassy, that would have come,
could have come, should have come
sooner, I concede.
Myself, answering, Sisyphus, son,
the lid coming down now
ash white,
better late than never answering, ending thus
this last refrain, jokester, prankster,
son, just a tiny crack left now:

It's all right.

III ✷ THE DRIFTING AWAY (1986)

The stars was shining, and the leaves rustled in the woods ever so mournful; and I heard an owl, away off, who-whooing about somebody that was dead, and a whip-porwill and a dog crying about somebody that was going to die, and the wind was trying to whisper something to me and I couldn't make out what it was . . .

—The Adventures of Huckleberry Finn

If I Could Open You

If I could open you, like
Einstein opened a hole
in the twentieth century,
that is what I would do.
When he realized what he
had done, I like to think he
sat there with his pencil, and
in his mind was a great, silver
city on a plain, and three
blue suns in the sky. And he
walked into that image then,
glad though terrified.

Unsent Message to My Brother in His Pain

Please do not die now. Listen.
Yesterday, storm clouds rolled
out of the west like thick muscles.
Lightning bloomed. Such a sideshow
of colors. You should have seen it.
A woman watched with me, then we slept.
Then, when I woke first, I saw
in her face that rest is possible.
The sky, it suddenly seems
important to tell you, the sky
was pink as a shell. Listen
to me. People orbit the moon now.
They must look like flies around
Fatty Arbuckle's head, that new
and that strange. My fellow American,
I bought a French cookbook. In it
are hundreds and hundreds of recipes.
If you come to see me, I shit you not,
we will cook with wine. Listen
to me. Listen to me, my brother,
please don't go. Take a later flight,
a later train. Another look around.

Chance of Showers

for Matt Horan

Like the greatest steak house
salad bar you ever saw, there is something
varied but, I am afraid, all
too familiar in this big autumnal air.

And yet, what other season
boils up such aches to get it down
precisely, hoping to avoid again
the always striking, but also fatal,

mention of the ornithological
V's on high. The trees seem the color
of fire trucks or blood or rust
again, but why? Why do we recall

the things we do? "Why did
the little moron take hay to bed?" I
don't suppose a week has passed
in thirty years I have not asked myself

that question. Why? Likewise
with Billy Pinzer. I was only
two, but every week I waddle out
on the porch once more, and see Billy

in the front yard, holding a little
yellow metal roadster. Ah Billy, he is
my buddy. He smiles at me. I
smile at him. I walk up to him. He hits

me in the face with the roadster.
Sometimes, when I peer out at my freshman
class, those seats of desolation,
or when I hear some Texan say something

particularly inane, I think
Billy is behind these bombs bursting
in here that, for an instant,
cause me to consider flipping through

advertisements in the back
of Argosy—to order a used, an actual
Colombian machete. "Imagine
the expressions on your friends' faces

as you cut a bloody swath
through the gang." For an instant.
Then I take another sip of coffee,
lean back and keep my mouth quite shut.

So does form give meaning
to memory. Does memory give meaning
to form? "Why yes!" cried crazy
Vera so long ago her face flared up

today from some recess where I
thought just narcosis reigned, miasmal
and malign. I got older this year,
and like black lightning from a blue sky

it surprised the hell out
of me. I don't think I could honestly

describe things as looking up,
but I can say they are still looking

not dull. Mortality, who
would have thought it? Maybe the best
to be hoped for is to pop off
in mid-melody, like Bach. These random

cameos, however, and tableaux
on parade appear preferable to even
the best of last refrains now.
For now. Now this glass wherein I see

myself lets me see other things
as well. That window in the far
wall, for instance, and outside
houses dripping gingerbread on the hill

across the street. If I squint
hard enough, they seem a rocky misty
blue-gray panorama, like
the inaccessible backgrounds of certain

Renaissance portraits of great
renown. Although I must say those craggy
backgrounds always made me think:
"That girl had better get going if she

wants to be home by dark."
Hogs are among us, no doubt about it,
no hedge against inflation
either. Ben Kimpel tells me things come

in cycles, I suppose that means
circles, and I guess that is a type
of good news, but I don't know, these
recollections seem constant, growing, one

long craggy protean scene,
and my bad knee gets worse every year,
I use it to forecast the weather
now, stuff to feed my nightmares and

daymares. My parents singing
"Always." While the shish kebab sellers,
on the corners and streets
of the world, are not moved to tears.

Day Begins at Governor's Square Mall

Here, newness is all. Or almost all. And like
a platterful of pope's noses at a White House dinner,
I exist apart. But these trees now—
how do you suppose they grow this high in here?
They look a little like the trees I sat beneath in 1959
waiting with my cheesecloth net for butterflies.
It was August and it was hot. Late summer,
yes, but already the leaves in trees were
flecked with ochers and the umbers of the dead.
I sweated there for hours, so driven,
so immersed in the forest's shimmering life,
that I could will my anxious self not move
for half a day—just on the imagined chance
of making some slight part of it my own.
Then they came. One perfect pair of just-hatched
black-and-white-striped butterflies. The white
lemon-tipped with light, in shade
then out, meandering. Zebra swallowtails,
floating, drunk in the sun, so rare to find
their narrow, fragile, two-inch tails intact.
At that moment I could only drop my net and stare.
The last of August. 1959. But these trees, now,
climb up through air and concrete never hot or cold.
And I suspect the last lepidopteran that found

themselves in here were sprayed then swept away.
Everyone is waiting though, as before a storm—
anticipating something. Do these leaves never fall?

Now, and with a mild surprise, faint
music falls. But no shop breaks open yet.
The people, like myself, range aimlessly;
the air seems thick and still. Then, lights blink on;
the escalators jerk and hum. And in the center, at
the exact center of the mall, a jet of water spurts
twenty feet straight up, then drops and spatters
in a shallow pool where signs announce that none
may ever go. O bright communion! O new cathedral!
where the appetitive, the impure, the old, the young,
the bored, the lost, the dumb, with wide dilated eyes
advance with offerings to be absolved and be made clean.
Now, the lime-lit chain-link fronts from over one hundred
pleasant and convenient stalls and stores are rolled away.
Now, odors of frying wontons come wafting up from
Lucy Ho's Bamboo Garden. And this music, always
everywhere, yet also somehow strangely played as if
not to be heard, pours its soft harangue down now.
The people wander forward now. And the world begins.

The Luncheon of the Boating Party

Under the red-and-white-striped awning
extended over the restaurant porch,
the eyelids of these fourteen sundry revelers

seem to sag a bit, and that is because
by now they are all just a little drunk.
The party is as parties are. The people

are talking. Laughing. But in the upper
left-hand corner, a man wearing
a saffron straw hat, tilted jauntily down

over his brow, stands slightly apart
and silent against the thin balustrade.
This man stands with his back arched,

his chest out, and the large muscles
in his bare arms self-consciously flexed.
Certainly, he cannot be at ease, but then those

who desperately hope to be loved rarely are.
I say this because if one follows
the man's gaze across the top of the canvas,

across the party, to the upper right-hand corner,
one sees that he is, I believe, staring
at a young woman who has raised her hands

to adjust her hat or her hair, or to cover her ears
so as not to hear what the two men talking
to her are saying. The two men are smiling,

and one has taken the liberty of slipping
his arm round her waist. The young woman
is the only person in the boating party being

physically touched, and though she seems
oblivious to it, the man in the saffron hat
is not, and is not much amused by it either.

Then, as the eye roams over the rest
of the festive scene, the quiet joke of the artist
begins to emerge. For, although a half dozen

conversations continue on, half of these people
are not even seeing the person looking at them.
They are looking at somebody else. It is a sort

of visual quadrille, the theme of five hundred
French farces, except in this case the painter
must care very much for them all, for he has soothed

their wants and aches in a wash of softness.
I think he must have been a little drunk too.
But it is the eyes, these misty, wine-dark eyes

of the three women in the center of the painting,
that draw a viewer back again and again.
The women are looking at men. They are looking

that way women sometimes look
when they have had a little wine, and when
they are listening to someone in whose presence

they see no reason to be other than who they are,
someone to whom, as a matter of fact,
they wish to communicate how simple and gentle

life can sometimes be, how amniotic even,
as it seems to them now. It is not clear
if the men of the boating party perceive this,

or anything. To be honest, they seem selfish and vain.
But the artist sees it. And this is his gift,
this warm afternoon, his funny story to tell again

and again: a day of blue grapes and black wine, of tricks
of the eye, of the flow and lulls of time, and everything,
everything soaked in the light of sex and love and the sun.

Morning Song

Flush and burn, your fever rose all night.
Your sleep was troubled; and even though I knew
This had to run its course, throughout the night
I tried but could not think of anything to do.
Often you cried out in that sleep, far away.
And wherever you were, I thought I could see
That whatever it was you kept wanting to say
It did not seem to have to do with me.

The tired eyes open. You see now that I see,
Swirling and tangled, inverted, how
In this firmament the blood streams and races.
Your smile and damp hair rush up to meet me,
Or is it I to them? This skin's blaze and glow—
The beads of dew on these most secret places.

The Lover Remembereth Such as He Sometime Enjoyed and Showeth How He Would Like to Enjoy Her Again

Luck is something I do not understand:
There were a lot of things I almost did
Last night. I almost went to hear a band
Down at The Swinging Door. I, almost, hid
Out in my room all night and read a book,
The Sot-Weed Factor, that I'd read before;
Almost, I drank a pint of Sunny Brook
I'd bought at the Dickson Street Liquor Store.

Instead I went to the Restaurant-On-The-Corner,
And tried to write, and did drink a beer or two.
Then coming back from getting rid of the beer,
I suddenly found I was looking straight at you.
Five months, my love, since I last touched your hand.
Luck is something I do not understand.

Adventures in Sepia

At the Will Rogers Court apartments
a young mother takes her toddler
into the living room to play,
then returns to the kitchen
to iron, and listen
to Stella Dallas on the radio.

Now the little one pushes at the front screen door,
finds it open, so stumbles out into the sun
where seven slightly older kids
come along, allowing him
to follow them
down the walk, down the road
to the old abandoned junior high
and the enormous, sunken, concrete storm drain there—
concrete smooth and cool,
concrete in the shade,
dark concrete the color
of Robert Oppenheimer's eyes
at any given moment in 1945.

The children climb down, scream, run around,
and so, with help, does the toddler too.
But then the older kids
climb out and run away,
climb out and leave the toddler alone.

The tips of his fingers can almost touch
the dead yellow grass
at the ground-level top of the drain.

Soon enough he sees
there is nothing to do
except sit down on concrete and cry.

Soon enough he feels
there is nothing on earth
for him but this gray
and that blue rectangular swatch of sky.

From far far down the black tube of Time
a man studies this scene
in light bronze.

A bronzed toddler is crying—
then looks up, seeing
first the head, then shoulders,
then the bronzed pedal pushers
of a bronzed mother there.
The man does not remember
the arms reaching up, or the arms reaching down,
just the distant sensation—
mendicant,
supplicant—

that he is risen,

that he inherits the air.

Semi-Sentimental Thank You Note Sent over a Long Distance

Let me tell you, I'm
    still trying to cope with
        the disappointment.
    All I wanted
for Christmas was
    a scratch-and-sniff
        photo of you
    amongst some clover.
Instead, this book
    of the fifty worst
        movies ever made.
    And a box of pink
erasers? Maybe I'm
    slow, but I don't
        get it. Oh yes, I
    know we are
separated by that
    enormously faded and
        dirty spread-out
    serape, that distinctive
state of mind, Oklahoma—
    but down here I am
        left mostly to
    my own devices. Here,
like Jackie Gleason's red
    satin bowling shirt,
        I lack subtlety
    and stand too much out

in the crowd. So
what I am getting at,
what I am trying
to say, my little
lotus blossom, my little
dove of Canaan, my
little garbanzo
bean, is thanks a lot
but I really must ask you
to get up off that
divine rotundity, your
ass, and send that
clever clover photo
right on down
the line right
now. There exists
a definite need! Like
Jackie Gleason's bowling
shirt, sooner
or later, I'm headed
your way, and when
I get back to Arkansas,
either to pick
you up or stay, let's
both plan on working
hard at, O ho, seeing
ah, eye to eye,
et al, and I might
add, toe to toe, et
al, nose to nose,
O, thigh to
thigh, et al,
ah, O, well, yes, O.

A Skeptical View of the Tarot

The Purveyor to the Czar attended a new exhibition
of post-impressionist efforts by Lonzo,
a recent twinkle in the art world sky.
The important official paused before
one painting, and said it gave *him*
the impression of the dried egg yellow
he found on his fork at breakfast that morning.
The next canvas, he said, gave him the impression
of his courtesan's black lace panties
lying on the carpet that afternoon,
a sour fog hovering over them, almost visible.

Lonzo, holding a skeptical view of the Tarot,
having, for the occasion, arrayed himself as The Fool
carrying a white rose and strolling over a cliff,
an ironic gesture of defiance,
heard these things.

As the purveyor continued his ridicule,
moving from painting to painting,
the locked stalls of the flaming mules
of melancholy were opened wide,
causing horrible screams to be heard in the land.
Then the artist was filled with dark choler,
saw the flaw in his gesture, and considered
that perhaps, after all, his chosen garb
did correctly express his archetype.

A Funny Joke

A man fell out of grace.
It was my father.

On the north slope of Alaska,
on land belonging to

the Atlantic-Richfield Oil Corporation,
he fell.

He lay there six hours.
Then he was found.

Three hours later,
the Atlantic-Richfield Oil Corporation

flew him to Fairbanks
where doctors were.

They said he was ill.
They said the way

his face, arm, leg, in fact
his whole left side

was drawn up
in a hideous, contorted,

spasm of paralysis
meant he was in ill health.

My brother was there.
My brother said

this was what was in my father's eyes:
fear.

My brother said
his mouth was twisted

into a permanent ghastly grin.
It looked always as if

his was the only smile around,
as if someone had told

the funniest joke finally,
but only he had heard

and we were unaware,
there, that last day

my father was an employee
of the Atlantic-Richfield Oil Corporation.

The Party's End

The moon steered a rusty car away.

We wandered into the backyard.

There was a little wind.

Someone sad whispered, "See,
now the poem of joy comes striding."

And I saw it then.

Why did it come then,
through that dirty horse night?

What visions came?

I saw my father working.
He bent and fell in Alaskan snow.

My brother also fell.

I wanted to touch them then.
I believe
I wanted to scream, "Help me,
God! Immensity!
Let me come unto you.
Let me come unto

you. Let me
come unto you."

But, of course,
none of us said anything.

The dawn was there.

And I was cold.

And all rage left me.

A frost had collected
on the shingles, and the grass,
so lovely
to my drunken eyes.

IV * OFTEN IN DIFFERENT LANDSCAPES (1976)

If this is tea, please bring me some coffee.
If this is coffee, please bring me some tea.

—Abraham Lincoln

To Laura Phelan: 1880–1906

for James Whitehead

Drunk I have been. And drunk I was that night
I lugged your stone across the other graves,
to set you up a hundred yards away.
Flowers I found, then. Drunk I have been.
And am, standing here with no moon to spill
on the letters of your name; my loud fingers
feeling them out. The stone is mossed over.
And why must I bring myself in the dark
to stand here among the sour grasses
that stain my white jeans? Drunk I have been.
See, the thick dew slides on the trees, wet weeds,
wetness smears the air; and a vague surf
of wildflowers pushes my feet, slipping
close to my legs. When the thought comes at last
that people fall apart, that the things we do
will not do. Ends. Then, we come to scenes
like this. This scene of you. You apart:
this is not you; and yet, this is where I stand
and close my eyes, and feel the ragged wind
blow red and maul my hair. In the night somewhere,
dandelions foam. This is not you. Drunk
I have been. Across this graveyard, that
is where you are. Yet I stand here. Would ask
things of your name. Would wish. Would not be told
of the stink in the skull, the eye's collapse.
Would be told something new, something unknown.—
A mosquito bites my hand. The only sound
is the rough wind. Drunk I have been,
here, at the loam's maw, before this stone
of yours, which is not you. Which is.

What the New Chef Said

"Those tapioca-type idiots
who come in here expecting
some kind of lethargic lull
to fill their puffed-out paunches
had damn better lift
their lardy asses up
and right on out the door. If
they hang long around here
I'll take a skewer
and stick the hogs, rotten
or not. What they want
is the old way, the old slow
metronome of flavors chopped
out and dropped on a plate
to set before the dunce.
That's over! All over!
Today's green salads
are the truly tossed
with sundry graffiti of zucchini
and weenie and bologna sprinkled
over all. I give the people
what the world is really like:
strawberry buttermilk
and prune pie. Ice
creams lost in sauerkraut.
That sweet-and-sour sauce
is what I make and
what I make is what (though
it bust their ulcerous guts)
what they devour!" he said.

California

Shouldn't we finally get going.
I mean I think the right time has come.
The wind drops the leaves to the ground.
I think we had better get going.
The sunrise, the sunrise has fallen.
The long rows of waves keep on coming.
They lap in the rocks by the shore.

I mean it is dusk on the shore.
And the wind kicks the leaves to the ground.
All over the black leaves are falling.
Why do we still only stand here?
The time for our starting has come.
Let us go to the boats and launch out.
I think it would be best to run.

What I mean is the sunrise is gone.
Let us run to the boats and start rowing.
The leaves, the leaves keep on falling.
The black leaves have covered the beaches.
And why do we still only stand here?
I mean why do we still only stand here?

The Murder of Gonzago and His Friends

In a district that's rarely traveled these days,
in a place where even the blackbirds lie down
in daylight, just north of West Fork,
I fell out with eight debauchees below some sycamores.
"Good fellows, arise!" I cried. "I
suspect you have heard the sad news."
But they were dull, sluggard, adamant, insane.
And besides, Mogen David seemed their chief concern.
The Arapahoes would soon be upon us: "Arise! Arise!
Shall blood-purple be the color of our pain?"
Nothing. Their eyes were not white rapids.
But no one could say I did not try. No one felt
I was to blame. No one. This was many years ago.
At night now, when I leave the house
with my jar of salt, my thoughts are of them. Each night
as I stand under my streetlight, I can think
only of them. And as I look down the long row
of streetlights, each with its own person,
holding his own jar, as I stand there
pouring salt on the slugs, that then blister and foam,
as I watch them dissolve, my thoughts are always of them.

Often in Different Landscapes

What should be done? No one knew for sure.
"Look at that chili-dog," I said to the blind guy,
after which I took it on the lam. The entire
offended countryside was up in arms. The Scourge
of Sheboygan the media labeled me. Those swine,
they forced me to the forests, taking shelter
in an abandoned hunting lodge. And only sometimes,
on the weekends, would I hear the snickering sounds
of couples in the woods. That first night, that
lonely night, the sleep dripped from my eyes,
was replaced by more, and rain dripped, and the dark
with its hard tonnage, I should add, also dripped,
oozing like hot asphalt under the door. Why
did it remind me so much of the blind guy
and his constant drool? My gorge rose. But not
for long. I packed those days with simple things,
taking up the Ace comb with cellophane, playing
songs of my own invention, such as "Johnny Belinda
Where Is Thy Sting," a personal favorite. But that, too,
sometimes brought thoughts of the blind guy, why
I don't know. And neither do I understand
where these recurring images come from, strange
images, often in different landscapes, and always
coming back, huge indigestions, to glut
my sleep, my waking moments, all my life
clogged with glossolalia, white canes, shrieks, slobber,
the spastic I tripped once behind the gym.

Little Keats Soliloquy

You're probably wondering
what I'm doing with this
2-by-4 said a stable boy,
and when I came to with
dried blood in my ear
I knew that I had
missed the joke again.
It happens all the time:
that was no refried banana
that was my wife. That
means something? Meant nothing
to me while they grinned
their asses off. You go
straight to hell I said;
but I can't go through
life this way, always outside
watching the baker
plopping pastries into
sacks for other kids,
that's no good, I know
that for sure, but what
can I do, what can I
use for a ladder, what
to carry me up into
the loft, away from these
stinking horses?

The Lamar Tech Football Team Has Won Its Game

The Lamar Tech football team has won its game.
My grandmother has died. The newspaper, yesterday,
Said, "Siamese Twins Cut Apart, One Lives." My father
Says, "Some things you have to learn to accept.
Take the good parts with the bad."
                    (This must be a dream.)
"Oh, yes," I say. "I remember how the sun feels warm
Even on the coldest days, sometimes."
The Lamar Tech football team.   The newspaper.

Belgium is now importing jukeboxes.
Australians are installing oil heaters.
Adversity is what makes you mature. "Oh, yes.
"I've seen the winter moon pumped up, platinum-like;
And the stars seem brightest when it's freezing."
Siamese twins.   On the coldest days, sometimes.
                    (This must be a dream.)
My father says, "Make hay while the sun shines."
The sun.   The moon.   Belgium is now importing
Jukeboxes.   One lives.   My father says, "In a few weeks
You'll feel better. Time is a great healer."   The sun.
The moon.
The Lamar Tech football team has won its game.

East Texas

The taste in my mouth
Was the taste of blood or rust on backdoor thermometers
Unread for twenty years. With my cheesecloth
Net I waited in the woods. Then the flutters
Of the giant swallowtails could be heard far away. Leaves
Moved. Sweat was acid in my eyes, and my father frowned
In his huge wheelchair. He could not get up the hill. My last two loves
Sat in pine straw, waiting to see what I would do. The sound
To my left was the sound of men standing at urinals.
But no. It was only the rain, uncontrollable, and the rain took
The gray shapes of steam. My father frowned. It was so steep.
And those shapes were the shapes of old women with shawls
On their heads, of old men sitting down. She shook
Me saying I was talking in my sleep.

To All Those Considering Coming to Fayetteville

Often these days, when my mind holds splinters
like the pieces of the Old Spice bottle
I dropped and shattered yesterday, I think
of other places. It is wintertime now,
and the Ozarks are hushed up with snow
everywhere. They are small mountains, almost
not mountains at all, but rather, with
trees sticking up, they seem more like
the white hairy bellies of fat old men
who have lain down here. What has this
to do with anything? I don't know. Except
it makes me think of snow elsewhere,
and what it would be like to be there. I
might drive across Oklahoma, then on
into New Mexico. I could be there tonight.
The land would be flat, the snow over
everything. The highway straight, and forever
the snow like blue cheese in the moonlight,
for as far as there is, and air, cold air
crisp as lettuce, wet lettuce in the store,
and I would keep driving, on and on.

Summer in Fairbanks

is like a dull dream. From time to time
the paperboy comes grinning with proof that
something has happened after all. Here
where the highways end. To go north
from here, you must be a bird or wealthy.
The prospectors have each been starved and strained
away down southward and to old folks homes.
Here is where the nights end too. Never
to sense the dark for days is strange, and not
so hot as one might think. It is strange
always to be able to see, and say:
that is there and that is there and that
is over there, always. Strange, not to tell
the end of days by any other way
than clocks, and meals; televisions turning off.
Different, for things to seem
to the eyes like one day, that somehow
has slowed down to months, years, icebergs
of minutes so separated by an absence
from anything that ever came before,
that the anxious people find themselves
waiting for the swish on their lime lawns
of the dirty tennis shoes of
the grinning paperboy who brings them yesterday.

The North Slope

Three months away from the word away from trees
and bushes hills newspapers women dark
on into the undeodorized the raw
twelve hours a day seven days a week
helicopters dropped us on tundra unrelieved
abandoned well sites to do away with
anything "environmentally unsound" there that
first day stacking scrap metal thinking the last words
of Scarlett O'Hara seeing how flat
the land was how brown how completely
unrelieved the flatness how raw the air
coming off the Arctic sea the horizon
a pencil line sometimes blending
with the frigid summer sky unrelieved
a foot and a half of tundra and under it
ice going down frozen earth eighteen hundred feet
I remember the small tundra flowers
delicate white blue the yellow poppies
in the second week I reached out to pick some
saw a jut of ice beside them
reaching up strange I shivered strange
something there I did not quite understand
could not get my mind around something
ice underneath them then back at base camp
before bed thought again and again
coldness what is it I thought strange unrelieved
more and more could not look at the flat
horizon or would not would keep my gaze away
from the white sky white fog the white

light from the sun never sinking what is it
I did not know only this feeling
someone walking always away something unsaid
and I kept my head down away from the sun the sky
then came the week of the caribou
the herds they came running unrelieved
thousands and thousands across the tundra
I kept my head down but at last could not
a hundred yards away two wolves loping behind
I saw them drag down a slow one
it was one hundred yards away
I saw them could not believe saw them
the red meadow of its side this was
one hundred yards away watched them eat
there was ice underground is ice
underground could not believe saw them rip ice
from its side ice the color of the sun I saw
it was raw it was nothing that fell from
its side ice emptiness came loping as birds
so many birds flew away and away screaming over
something they seemed to have heard
unrelieved the sound now of blood falling
of ice now and of whaleboats I could not believe
thinking her last words what was it the birds said
going away what was it the ice whispered raw
could not lift my head
the jet trails sagged over Dead Horse
and drifted away here where you aim
the harpoon sailor see it surface see it wallow
unrelieved see it dive here where the wait is
the ache for anything anything not dropping away
she breaches she breaches they cried and that
image charging my head all that white reaching

up that vacuum revealed unrelieved
and the froth all the spray and it sinking back
under leaving me asking for some other thing
for some other way asking time
to turn to forget what is there what is not
everywhere birds kept flying away
but Scarlett Scarlett this is the place
where tomorrow never comes the sun like
red ice searing always the summer the land
of absence of nothing of cold of no night
the wind blowing frozen off the Arctic sea

The Polar Bear

In the only land where things are truly white
The polar bear is too. He lumbers about,
His round, white stomach full of fish.
The meat of the fish lies white inside him;
His thick, shaggy coat shines white in the sun.
And as he moves over snow and ice,
He slips out of sight before our eyes
In an almost magical blending of light.

And the polar bear has this land to himself.
All to himself he roams the ice;
For very few creatures, and fewer men,
Can live with the always unbending of white.

Like no man I know of, he sleeps at night
With his stomach, and dreams, full of white.

But Once in Special

Get out of here with your ideas about
going downtown to see that roller coaster
and no I do not want to buy any more
ping pong balls now look this is my room
I pay the rent so please remove
these midgets and try to understand
it's nothing personal actually I've
always liked shorter Get away from that
aquarium if you don't mind God damn
people this is well OK see it was
the other day or maybe last year
I don't remember too clearly anymore
I slid into this out of sight witch
her dark eyes sadder than the sea
try to understand when she moved the air
flowed out in waves before her and she moved
so softly those waves they still keep rolling over me

Gifts

They say that blood is salt. I've
tasted yours, and they are right.
So let's get on with our big painting
exchange. In mine, I've placed you
in a black pasture, with black horses,
your red eyes clearly discerned. But,
and I observe you're having the same
problem, here in the middle distance
isn't really the right place for you
somehow. Over more to the left,
I think, yes, under that smeared vision
of crows, way out in those dark, waist-high
weeds, there, leaning against that
huge pile of horseshit, yes, and a little
nearer the vanishing point, thank you.

Religious Poem

A Shakespearean dusk in November.
Bleak scenes. Bone trees, and so on.
Let my many gargoyle faces come whirling!
Oh, which to choose? Shall it be Paul Scofield
as Sir Thomas More? Jesus no! Or how about
Jesus? That's one I've done. Of course I
never admitted it was Jesus; and often I
would change the appearance, so it looked like
someone besides Jesus. After all, if
people saw a person going around with
the face of Jesus on, well, that would be
a little self-indulgent. I mean, Jesus
is a deity and everything; some people
might see it as a sacrilege. Anyone might.
You have to be real careful. I
Argued with myself, and so on, and on.

This Other

Your self confronts you at the oddest times.
    Not too often, but often at odd times,
this other bangs through the front door, catching
    you tired and at supper, but still in your black
cape and doublet, tired, of imagining
    knowing, of imagining gesturing
hypnotically from the battlements—
    and your dinner becomes an interrupted
dinner, as he sits down and digs into
    the roast duck, orange sauce, the red Bordeaux.

You think: what a strange fellow. A healthy
    appetite, but the little paper pirate hat
sitting on his head, the kind in the dime stores
    around Halloween, would put most people off.
He eats with his hands. Quickly. And yet,
    there is something about this ruffian,
something about this greasy gorilla,
    something about this person with a penchant
for orange sauce, that makes you think: here is one
    with which I might dine; one with I might
lift a fine glass; one with which I might speak.

To His Book

Wafer; thin and hard and bitter pill I
    Take from time to time; pillow I have lain
        Too long on; holding the brief dreams, the styled
Dreams, the nightmares, shadows, red flames high
    High up on mountains; wilted zinnias, rain
        On dust, and great weight, the dead dog, and wild
Onions; mastodonic woman who knows how—
    I'm tired of you, tired of your insane
        Acid eating in the brain. Sharp stones, piled
Particularly, I let you go. Sink, or float, or fly now,
                    Bad child.